Market Dynamics

A Comprehensive Guide to Building brands and Driving Success

By

Taylor Caldwell

Copyright ©2024 by Taylor Caldwell

All right reserved. No part of this book may be used or reproduced in any form whatsoever without written permission except in the case of brief quotation in critical article or reviews

Book design by (Taylor Caldwell)
Cover design by (Taylor Caldwell)

First Edition: month 2024

Table of contents

Introduction

Chapter 1
- Introduction

Chapter 2
- Supply and Demand

Chapter 3
- Competition

Chapter 4
- Consumer Behavior

Chapter 5
- Technological Advancements

Chapter 6
- Regulatory Changes

Chapter 7
- Economic Trends

Chapter 8
- Globalization

Chapter 9
- Sustainability

Chapter 10
- Forecasting Market Dynamics

Chapter 11
- Market Dynamics in Action

Chapter 12
- The Future of Market Dynamics

Conclusion

Introduction

Welcome to "Market Dynamics: Navigating the Forces Shaping Our Economic Landscape." In this comprehensive exploration, we delve into the intricate interplay of factors that drive and define our markets. From the timeless principles of supply and demand to the disruptive influence of technological advancements, this book offers a holistic perspective on the ever-evolving world of commerce.

Chapter 1 lays the groundwork with an Introduction, setting the stage for our journey into the heart of market dynamics. We then proceed to unravel the fundamental principles of Supply and Demand in Chapter 2, exploring how the delicate balance between these two forces shapes pricing, production, and distribution.

Competition takes center stage in Chapter 3, as we dissect the strategies and tactics employed by businesses to gain a competitive edge in crowded marketplaces. Chapter 4 delves into Consumer Behavior, offering insights into the psychology and decision-making processes that drive purchasing habits.

In Chapter 5, we examine the transformative power of Technological Advancements, from the advent of e-commerce to the rise of artificial intelligence, and their profound implications for industries and consumers alike. Regulatory Changes take the spotlight in Chapter 6, as we analyze the impact of laws and policies on market dynamics.

Chapter 7 shines a light on Economic Trends, exploring the cyclical nature of economies and the factors that influence growth and recession. Globalization takes center stage in Chapter 8, as we explore the interconnectedness of markets across borders and continents.

Sustainability emerges as a critical theme in Chapter 9, as we investigate the growing importance of ethical and environmental considerations in business practices. Chapter 10 equips readers with the tools for Forecasting Market Dynamics, empowering them to anticipate and adapt to shifting trends.

In Chapter 11, we bring theory into practice with real-world examples of Market Dynamics in Action, showcasing how businesses and industries respond to changing conditions. Finally, Chapter 12 peers into The Future of Market Dynamics, speculating on emerging trends and potential disruptions that will shape tomorrow's markets.

Whether you're a seasoned economist, a budding entrepreneur, or simply a curious observer of the global economy, "Market Dynamics" offers a comprehensive guide to understanding and navigating the complex forces that drive our markets forward. Join us on this enlightening journey as we uncover the dynamics that shape our economic landscape.

Chapter 1

Introduction

Welcome to the fascinating world of market dynamics. In this inaugural chapter, we embark on a journey to explore the intricate web of forces that shape our economic landscape. From the bustling markets of local communities to the sprawling global marketplace, understanding market dynamics is crucial for navigating the complexities of commerce.

At its core, market dynamics encapsulates the ever-changing interactions between buyers and sellers, producers and consumers, regulators and innovators. It encompasses a myriad of factors, from the basic principles of supply and demand to the nuances of consumer behavior and the broader influences of technology, regulation, and globalization.

In the pages that follow, we will unravel the mysteries of market dynamics, seeking to decipher the underlying mechanisms that drive fluctuations in prices, shifts in demand, and the rise and fall of industries. But before we dive into the details, it's essential to establish a foundational understanding of what exactly constitutes market dynamics and why it matters.

Market dynamics is not a static concept but rather a fluid and dynamic phenomenon. It encompasses the ebb and flow of economic activity, influenced by a multitude of internal and external factors. At its heart lies the interplay between supply and demand, the foundational forces that dictate the allocation of resources and the determination of prices in a market economy.

However, market dynamics extend far beyond the simple interaction of buyers and sellers. They are shaped by a complex interplay of factors, including competition among firms, changes in consumer preferences, technological innovations, regulatory interventions, economic trends, and the inexorable march of globalization.

Understanding market dynamics is essential for businesses seeking to thrive in today's fast-paced and ever-changing marketplace. By grasping the underlying principles and trends that govern market behavior, firms can anticipate shifts in demand, identify emerging opportunities, and adapt their strategies accordingly.

Moreover, market dynamics have profound implications for policymakers, regulators, and society as a whole. By understanding the forces at play in our markets, policymakers can craft more effective policies to promote competition, innovation, and consumer welfare. Similarly, by staying attuned to market dynamics, consumers can make informed decisions that align with their preferences and values.

As we journey through the chapters ahead, we will delve deeper into the various facets of market dynamics, exploring each component in detail and examining its implications for businesses, consumers, and society. By the end of this book, readers will emerge with a comprehensive understanding of the forces shaping our economic landscape and the tools to navigate them effectively.

So, join us as we embark on this enlightening exploration of market dynamics, where theory meets practice, and insights abound. Together, let's uncover the secrets of our dynamic markets and unlock the keys to success in an ever-changing world.

Chapter 2

Supply and Demand

In this chapter, we delve into the foundational principles of supply and demand, which form the bedrock of market dynamics. Understanding the dynamics of supply and demand is essential for grasping how prices are determined, how resources are allocated, and how markets function.

Supply refers to the quantity of a good or service that producers are willing and able to offer for sale at various prices during a given period. It is influenced by factors such as production costs, technological advancements, and the availability of inputs. The law of supply states that, all else being equal, as the price of a good or service rises, the quantity supplied increases, and vice versa. This positive relationship between price and quantity supplied is represented by the upward-sloping supply curve.

Demand, on the other hand, refers to the quantity of a good or service that consumers are willing and able to purchase at various prices during a given period. It is influenced by factors such as consumer preferences, income levels, and the prices of related goods. The law of demand states that, all else being equal, as the price of a good or service rises, the quantity demanded decreases, and vice versa. This inverse relationship between price and quantity demanded is represented by the downward-sloping demand curve.

The intersection of the supply and demand curves determines the equilibrium price and quantity in a market. At this point, the quantity supplied equals the quantity demanded, leading to market equilibrium. Any deviation from this equilibrium leads to a situation of either excess supply (surplus) or excess demand (shortage), which exerts pressure on prices and prompts adjustments in the market.

Changes in supply and demand can result from various factors, including shifts in consumer preferences, changes in input prices, technological advancements, and shifts in income levels. These changes can cause shifts in the supply and demand curves, leading to changes in equilibrium price and quantity.

Understanding supply and demand dynamics enables businesses to make informed decisions about pricing, production levels, and resource allocation. By anticipating changes in supply and demand, firms can adjust their strategies to maximize profitability and respond effectively to shifts in market conditions.

Moreover, policymakers can utilize supply and demand analysis to design and implement effective policies aimed at achieving specific economic outcomes. For example, policies that affect production costs or consumer incomes can influence supply and demand dynamics, with implications for prices, quantities, and overall market welfare.

In summary, supply and demand are the fundamental drivers of market dynamics, shaping prices, quantities, and resource allocation in markets. By understanding the principles of supply and demand and their interactions, businesses, policymakers, and consumers can navigate the complexities of markets more effectively and achieve their objectives.

Chapter 3

Competition

Competition is a cornerstone of market dynamics, driving innovation, efficiency, and consumer welfare. In this chapter, we explore the various forms of competition and their implications for market outcomes.

Competition occurs when multiple firms vie for the same customers by offering similar goods or services. It fosters efficiency by incentivizing firms to reduce costs, improve quality, and innovate in order to gain a competitive edge. Moreover, competition encourages firms to respond to consumer preferences and market signals, leading to greater diversity and choice for consumers.

There are several forms of competition, ranging from perfect competition to monopoly. Perfect competition is characterized by many small firms producing identical goods or services, with no single firm able to influence market prices. In contrast, monopoly exists when a single firm dominates the market, allowing it to control prices and quantities with little or no competition. Between these extremes lie various forms of imperfect competition, such as monopolistic competition and oligopoly, where a few firms dominate the market to varying degrees.

Competition can take place on multiple levels, including price competition, non-price competition, and strategic competition. Price competition involves firms competing primarily on the basis of price, often leading to price wars and downward pressure on prices. Non-price competition, on the other hand, focuses on factors other than price, such as product differentiation, branding, and customer service. Strategic competition involves firms engaging in strategic maneuvers, such as mergers, acquisitions, and alliances, to gain a competitive advantage.

Competition is regulated by antitrust laws and competition policies aimed at promoting fair competition and preventing anti-competitive practices. These laws and policies seek to protect consumers from monopolistic behavior, ensure a level playing field for firms, and promote innovation and efficiency in markets.

Despite its benefits, competition can also pose challenges for firms, particularly smaller businesses that may struggle to compete with larger, more established competitors. Moreover, intense competition can lead to market saturation, price volatility, and reduced profitability for firms.

Overall, competition is a driving force in market dynamics, shaping prices, quantities, and market structure. By understanding the nature of competition and its implications for market outcomes, businesses, policymakers, and consumers can make more informed decisions and contribute to the dynamism and vibrancy of markets.

Chapter 4

Consumer Behavior

Consumer behavior is a critical aspect of market dynamics, influencing purchasing decisions, demand patterns, and market outcomes. In this chapter, we delve into the factors that shape consumer behavior and their implications for businesses and markets.

Consumer behavior encompasses the actions, preferences, and decision-making processes of individuals or households when purchasing goods or services. It is influenced by a myriad of factors, including psychological, social, cultural, and economic variables.

One of the key determinants of consumer behavior is utility maximization, whereby consumers seek to maximize their satisfaction or utility from the goods and services they consume. This can involve considerations such as price, quality, convenience, and personal preferences.

Psychological factors also play a significant role in shaping consumer behavior. These include perception, attitudes, beliefs, and emotions, which can influence how consumers perceive and evaluate products, brands, and marketing messages.

Social and cultural factors exert a powerful influence on consumer behavior as well. Social influences, such as peer pressure, social norms, and reference groups, can affect consumers' purchasing decisions and consumption patterns. Cultural factors, including values, beliefs, and traditions, shape consumers' preferences and consumption habits across different societies and cultures.

Economic variables, such as income, wealth, and price sensitivity, also play a crucial role in determining consumer behavior. Changes in these variables can impact consumers' purchasing power and propensity to buy certain goods or services.

Understanding consumer behavior is essential for businesses seeking to effectively target and appeal to their target market. By understanding consumers' needs, wants, and preferences, firms can develop products, services, and marketing strategies that resonate with their target audience.

Moreover, consumer behavior has implications for market outcomes, including demand patterns, pricing strategies, and market dynamics. Changes in consumer behavior can lead to shifts in demand for certain products or services, creating opportunities or challenges for businesses operating in those markets.

Policymakers and regulators also take consumer behavior into account when designing and implementing policies aimed at protecting consumers' interests and promoting market efficiency. For example, consumer protection laws may be enacted to ensure fair and transparent business practices, while advertising regulations may be implemented to prevent deceptive or misleading marketing tactics.

In summary, consumer behavior is a multifaceted phenomenon that influences market dynamics in profound ways. By understanding the factors that shape consumer behavior and their implications for businesses and markets, stakeholders can make more informed decisions and contribute to the overall efficiency and effectiveness of markets.

Chapter 5

Technological Advancements

Technological advancements play a pivotal role in shaping market dynamics, revolutionizing industries, and transforming the way businesses operate. In this chapter, we explore the impact of technological innovations on markets and economies.

Technological advancements encompass a wide range of innovations, from breakthroughs in information technology to advancements in manufacturing processes, transportation, communication, and beyond. These advancements drive productivity growth, spur innovation, and open up new opportunities for businesses and consumers alike.

One of the key ways in which technological advancements influence market dynamics is through increased efficiency and productivity. Automation, robotics, and digitalization streamline production processes, reduce costs, and enhance the quality and consistency of goods and services. This increased efficiency translates into lower prices for consumers, higher profits for businesses, and overall economic growth.

Moreover, technological advancements enable businesses to innovate and differentiate themselves in the marketplace. From the development of new products and services to the creation of novel business models and distribution channels, technology empowers firms to stay ahead of the competition and meet the evolving needs and preferences of consumers.

The rise of the internet and digital technologies has also revolutionized the way businesses interact with consumers and markets. E-commerce platforms, social media, and digital marketing tools have opened up new channels for reaching customers, expanding market reach, and gathering data on consumer behavior. These digital technologies have leveled the playing field for businesses of all sizes, enabling startups and small businesses to compete with larger, more established players.

Technological advancements have also facilitated the emergence of new industries and business models, disrupting traditional markets and creating new opportunities for growth and innovation. From the sharing economy to the rise of artificial intelligence and blockchain technology, these innovations are reshaping industries such as transportation, finance, healthcare, and beyond.

However, technological advancements also pose challenges and risks, including job displacement, income inequality, and concerns about data privacy and cybersecurity. As technology continues to evolve at a rapid pace, policymakers, businesses, and society as a whole must grapple with these challenges and ensure that the benefits of technological progress are shared equitably across all segments of society.

In summary, technological advancements are a driving force behind market dynamics, shaping industries, businesses, and consumer behavior in profound ways. By embracing innovation, adapting to technological change, and leveraging new opportunities, businesses and economies can thrive in an increasingly digital and interconnected world.

Chapter 6

Regulatory Changes

Regulatory changes are a significant driver of market dynamics, shaping the operating environment for businesses, influencing consumer behavior, and impacting market outcomes. In this chapter, we explore the role of regulations in markets and economies.

Regulations encompass a wide range of rules, laws, and policies enacted by governments at the local, national, and international levels. These regulations are designed to achieve various objectives, including protecting consumers, promoting competition, ensuring financial stability, and safeguarding the environment.

One of the primary goals of regulations is to protect consumers from harmful or unfair business practices. Consumer protection regulations may include laws governing product safety, labeling requirements, and advertising standards, aimed at ensuring that consumers have access to accurate information and safe products.

Regulations also play a crucial role in promoting competition and preventing anti-competitive behavior in markets. Antitrust laws and competition policies are designed to prevent monopolies, cartels, and other forms of market power that can distort competition, harm consumers, and inhibit innovation.

Financial regulations are another important aspect of regulatory changes, aimed at ensuring the stability and integrity of financial markets. These regulations may include measures such as capital requirements, risk management standards, and oversight of financial institutions to mitigate systemic risks and prevent financial crises.

Environmental regulations are becoming increasingly important in addressing environmental challenges such as pollution, climate change, and resource depletion. These regulations may include emission standards, renewable energy targets, and conservation measures aimed at promoting sustainable practices and reducing environmental impact.

Technological advancements also pose new regulatory challenges, particularly in areas such as data privacy, cybersecurity, and emerging technologies like artificial intelligence and biotechnology. Policymakers must grapple with these challenges and adapt regulations to address the evolving risks and opportunities presented by technological innovation.

Regulatory changes can have profound implications for businesses, influencing their operations, strategies, and bottom line. Compliance with regulations may require businesses to invest in new technologies, adopt new practices, or modify their products and services to meet regulatory standards.

Moreover, regulatory changes can also impact consumer behavior, influencing purchasing decisions, brand perceptions, and market demand. For example, regulations requiring the disclosure of nutritional information on food packaging may influence consumers' choices and preferences.

In summary, regulatory changes are a critical aspect of market dynamics, shaping the legal and institutional framework within which businesses operate and markets function. By understanding the role of regulations in markets and economies, stakeholders can navigate regulatory changes more effectively and contribute to the overall efficiency and stability of markets.

Chapter 7

Economic Trends

Economic trends are a key driver of market dynamics, influencing business cycles, consumer behavior, and market outcomes. In this chapter, we explore the various economic trends that shape markets and economies.

Economic trends refer to the direction and magnitude of changes in key economic indicators over time. These indicators include measures such as gross domestic product (GDP), inflation, unemployment, interest rates, and consumer confidence. By analyzing these indicators, economists and policymakers can gain insights into the health and trajectory of an economy.

One of the most closely watched economic trends is economic growth, as measured by changes in GDP. Economic growth reflects the overall expansion of an economy's output of goods and services over time and is a key determinant of living standards and prosperity. Positive economic growth can stimulate consumer spending, business investment, and job creation, leading to increased demand and market activity.

Inflation is another important economic trend that influences market dynamics. Inflation refers to the rate at which the general level of prices for goods and services is rising. Moderate inflation is generally considered healthy for an economy, as it signals increasing demand and growth. However, high or persistent inflation can erode purchasing power, reduce consumer confidence, and lead to economic instability.

Unemployment is a closely watched economic indicator that reflects the health of the labor market. High unemployment rates can dampen consumer spending and confidence, leading to decreased demand for goods and services and slowing economic growth. Conversely, low unemployment rates can stimulate consumer spending and investment, driving economic expansion.

Interest rates are a critical economic trend that influences borrowing and investment decisions, as well as consumer spending. Central banks use interest rates as a tool to control inflation and stimulate economic activity. Lowering interest rates can stimulate borrowing and investment, while raising interest rates can help cool inflationary pressures.

Consumer confidence is a key indicator of consumer sentiment and spending intentions. High consumer confidence indicates optimism about the economy and future prospects, leading to increased consumer spending and economic growth. Conversely, low consumer confidence can dampen spending and economic activity.

Global economic trends also play a significant role in shaping market dynamics, as economies around the world become increasingly interconnected. Trends such as international trade flows, exchange rates, and geopolitical developments can impact market sentiment, business operations, and investment decisions.

Understanding economic trends is essential for businesses, policymakers, and investors seeking to navigate market dynamics and make informed decisions. By monitoring key economic indicators and trends, stakeholders can anticipate changes in market conditions, identify opportunities, and mitigate risks.

In summary, economic trends are a crucial driver of market dynamics, shaping business cycles, consumer behavior, and market outcomes. By understanding the various economic indicators and trends that influence markets and economies, stakeholders can better navigate the complexities of the marketplace and position themselves for success.

Chapter 8

Globalization

Globalization is a transformative force that has profoundly impacted market dynamics, reshaping industries, supply chains, and consumer preferences on a global scale. In this chapter, we explore the drivers, challenges, and implications of globalization for businesses and markets.

Globalization refers to the increasing interconnectedness and interdependence of economies around the world, facilitated by advances in technology, communication, and transportation. It has led to the expansion of international trade, investment, and migration, creating a more integrated and interconnected global marketplace.

One of the key drivers of globalization is technological advancement, which has dramatically reduced the cost and barriers to communication and transportation. The internet, digital technologies, and global supply chains have enabled businesses to reach new markets, collaborate with partners across borders, and access resources and talent from around the world.

Trade liberalization and economic reforms have also played a significant role in driving globalization. Tariff reductions, trade agreements, and deregulation have facilitated the flow of goods, services, and capital across borders, opening up new opportunities for businesses to expand their operations and reach new customers.

Globalization has led to the emergence of global supply chains, where components and production processes are spread across multiple countries. This has enabled businesses to access lower-cost inputs, increase efficiency, and respond more quickly to changes in market demand. However, it has also increased the complexity and vulnerability of supply chains, as demonstrated by disruptions such as the COVID-19 pandemic.

Globalization has also transformed consumer preferences and behavior, leading to the rise of global brands, cultural homogenization, and the spread of Western consumer culture around the world. Consumers now have access to a wider array of products and services from different countries and cultures, leading to increased competition and choice in the marketplace.

While globalization has brought about many benefits, it has also posed challenges and risks for businesses and markets. These include increased competition from foreign competitors, exposure to exchange rate fluctuations, regulatory differences across countries, and geopolitical tensions.

Moreover, globalization has raised concerns about income inequality, job displacement, and the impact of trade on workers and communities. Critics argue that globalization has led to the outsourcing of jobs to low-wage countries, undermining wages and labor standards in developed countries.

In response to these challenges, policymakers and businesses must adopt strategies to navigate the complexities of globalization effectively. This may involve investing in workforce training and education, diversifying supply chains, leveraging technology to enhance competitiveness, and engaging in responsible business practices that promote sustainability and social responsibility.

In summary, globalization is a transformative force that has reshaped markets, industries, and economies around the world. By understanding the drivers, challenges, and implications of globalization, businesses and policymakers can harness its opportunities while mitigating its risks, contributing to a more prosperous and sustainable global marketplace.

Chapter 9

Sustainability

Sustainability has emerged as a critical consideration in market dynamics, reflecting growing awareness of environmental and social issues and the need for businesses to operate in a responsible and sustainable manner. In this chapter, we explore the importance of sustainability in markets and economies and its implications for businesses and society.

Sustainability encompasses the concept of meeting the needs of the present without compromising the ability of future generations to meet their own needs. It involves balancing economic growth, social equity, and environmental stewardship to ensure long-term prosperity and well-being for all.

One of the key drivers of sustainability is growing recognition of the environmental challenges facing our planet, including climate change, pollution, deforestation, and depletion of natural resources. Businesses are increasingly under pressure to reduce their environmental footprint, minimize waste, and adopt sustainable practices throughout their operations.

Consumer demand for sustainable products and services is also driving businesses to prioritize sustainability. Studies show that a growing number of consumers are willing to pay a premium for products and services that are environmentally friendly, ethically sourced, and produced in a socially responsible manner. Businesses that fail to meet these expectations risk losing market share and facing reputational damage.

Moreover, regulatory pressures and government policies aimed at addressing environmental and social issues are shaping market dynamics. These may include emissions regulations, waste management laws, and incentives for renewable energy and sustainable practices. By aligning with these regulations and policies, businesses can mitigate risks and capitalize on opportunities in the growing market for sustainable products and services.

Sustainability extends beyond environmental considerations to encompass social and economic dimensions as well. Businesses are increasingly expected to address issues such as labor rights, human rights, diversity and inclusion, and community engagement. By promoting fair labor practices, supporting local communities, and fostering diversity and inclusion, businesses can enhance their reputation, build trust with stakeholders, and create long-term value.

Embracing sustainability can also lead to business benefits such as cost savings, innovation, and enhanced brand loyalty. Sustainable practices such as energy efficiency, waste reduction, and supply chain transparency can result in lower operating costs and improved efficiency. Moreover, sustainability can drive innovation by encouraging businesses to develop new products, services, and business models that address societal and environmental challenges.

In summary, sustainability is a critical consideration in market dynamics, influencing consumer preferences, regulatory trends, and business strategies. By embracing sustainability, businesses can enhance their competitiveness, mitigate risks, and contribute to a more sustainable and prosperous future for all.

Chapter 10

Forecasting Market Dynamics

Forecasting market dynamics is essential for businesses, policymakers, and investors seeking to anticipate and adapt to changes in market conditions. In this chapter, we explore the various methods and tools used to forecast market dynamics and their implications for decision-making.

Forecasting market dynamics involves predicting future trends and developments in key market indicators such as prices, demand, supply, and competition. By understanding how these factors are likely to evolve over time, stakeholders can make more informed decisions about resource allocation, pricing strategies, and risk management.

One of the most commonly used methods for forecasting market dynamics is statistical analysis, which involves analyzing historical data to identify patterns and trends. Time series analysis, regression analysis, and econometric modeling are examples of statistical techniques used to forecast market variables such as sales, prices, and economic indicators.

Another approach to forecasting market dynamics is qualitative analysis, which involves gathering insights and opinions from experts, stakeholders, and industry insiders. Qualitative methods such as surveys, interviews, and expert panels can provide valuable insights into future market trends, consumer preferences, and industry developments that may not be captured by quantitative data alone.

Scenario analysis is another useful tool for forecasting market dynamics, particularly in uncertain or volatile environments. Scenario analysis involves developing multiple hypothetical scenarios based on different assumptions and assessing the potential outcomes and implications of each scenario. This can help stakeholders prepare for a range of possible future outcomes and develop contingency plans accordingly.

Technological advancements have also enabled the use of more sophisticated forecasting methods, such as machine learning and artificial intelligence. These techniques involve training algorithms to analyze large volumes of data and identify patterns and relationships that may not be apparent to human analysts. Machine learning algorithms can be used to forecast market variables such as consumer behavior, demand patterns, and price movements with a high degree of accuracy.

While forecasting market dynamics can provide valuable insights and inform decision-making, it is important to recognize the limitations and uncertainties inherent in any forecasting exercise. Market dynamics are influenced by a wide range of factors, including economic trends, technological advancements, regulatory changes, and unforeseen events such as natural disasters or pandemics. As such, forecasts should be treated as probabilistic estimates rather than precise predictions of future outcomes.

Moreover, forecasting errors and biases can occur due to factors such as data limitations, model assumptions, and human judgment. It is important for forecasters to carefully consider the assumptions underlying their forecasts, validate their models against historical data, and incorporate feedback and adjustments as new information becomes available.

In summary, forecasting market dynamics is a valuable tool for businesses, policymakers, and investors seeking to anticipate and adapt to changes in market conditions. By employing a combination of quantitative and qualitative methods, leveraging technological advancements, and recognizing the inherent uncertainties and limitations of forecasting, stakeholders can make more informed decisions and navigate the complexities of the marketplace more effectively.

Chapter 11

Market Dynamics in Action

In this chapter, we examine real-world examples of market dynamics in action, showcasing how businesses and industries respond to changing conditions, competition, and consumer preferences. By studying these case studies, we gain insights into the dynamics that shape markets and the strategies employed by stakeholders to navigate them effectively.

1. Disruptive Innovation: The rise of companies like Uber and Airbnb illustrates the power of disruptive innovation in reshaping industries and challenging traditional business models. By leveraging technology and tapping into underutilized resources, these companies have transformed transportation and accommodation markets, creating new opportunities for consumers and posing challenges for incumbents.

2. Industry Consolidation: Mergers and acquisitions are common strategies used by businesses to consolidate market power, expand market share, and achieve economies of scale. Examples include the merger of Disney and Fox in the entertainment industry and the acquisition of Whole Foods by Amazon in the retail sector. These moves can lead to increased efficiency and competitiveness but may also raise concerns about market concentration and anticompetitive behavior.

3. Platform Economy: The emergence of platform-based business models, such as Amazon, Google, and Facebook, has fundamentally altered the dynamics of markets across various industries. These platforms connect buyers and sellers, facilitate transactions, and generate vast amounts of data that can be leveraged for targeted advertising and personalized services. However, concerns about data privacy, market dominance, and regulatory oversight have accompanied the rapid growth of platform economies.

4. Global Supply Chains: The COVID-19 pandemic exposed vulnerabilities in global supply chains, disrupting production, distribution, and logistics networks

around the world. Companies faced challenges such as shortages of raw materials, disruptions in transportation, and shifts in consumer demand. As a result, many businesses have begun reevaluating their supply chain strategies, diversifying sourcing, and adopting technologies to enhance resilience and agility.

5. Sustainability Initiatives: Increasingly, businesses are incorporating sustainability into their operations and strategies in response to growing consumer demand, regulatory pressures, and environmental concerns. Companies like Patagonia and Unilever have made sustainability a core part of their business models, investing in renewable energy, reducing waste, and promoting ethical sourcing and labor practices. These initiatives not only benefit the environment but also enhance brand reputation and customer loyalty.

6. E-commerce Boom: The rapid growth of e-commerce has transformed the retail landscape, disrupting traditional brick-and-mortar stores and driving significant shifts in consumer behavior. Companies like Amazon have capitalized on changing consumer preferences for online shopping, offering convenience, choice, and competitive prices. This trend has forced traditional retailers to adapt, invest in digital capabilities, and develop omnichannel strategies to remain competitive in an increasingly digital marketplace.

These examples illustrate the dynamic nature of markets and the myriad factors that shape their evolution. By studying real-world cases of market dynamics in action, businesses, policymakers, and investors can glean valuable insights into emerging trends, competitive strategies, and best practices for navigating the complexities of the marketplace.

Chapter 12

The Future of Market Dynamics

In this final chapter, we peer into the crystal ball to speculate on the future of market dynamics. While the future is inherently uncertain, several trends and developments are likely to shape the evolution of markets and economies in the years to come. By exploring these trends, we can gain insights into the opportunities and challenges that lie ahead and prepare ourselves to navigate the future marketplace effectively.

1. Digital Transformation: The pace of digital transformation is expected to accelerate, driven by advances in technologies such as artificial intelligence, internet of things (IoT), and blockchain. These technologies will continue to reshape industries, business models, and consumer experiences, leading to increased automation, customization, and connectivity across markets.

2. Sustainability Imperative: Sustainability will become an even more prominent consideration in market dynamics, driven by growing environmental concerns, regulatory pressures, and shifting consumer preferences. Businesses will increasingly adopt sustainable practices throughout their operations, supply chains, and product offerings, in response to stakeholder demands and market forces.

3. Resilient Supply Chains: The COVID-19 pandemic has underscored the importance of resilient supply chains capable of withstanding disruptions and shocks. Businesses will prioritize supply chain resilience, diversifying sourcing, investing in digital technologies, and adopting agile and flexible supply chain strategies to mitigate risks and enhance responsiveness.

4. Shifts in Consumer Behavior: Consumer behavior will continue to evolve in response to technological advancements, demographic changes, and societal trends. The rise of digital natives, changing demographics, and shifting cultural

norms will shape consumer preferences and consumption patterns, creating new opportunities and challenges for businesses.

5. Rise of Emerging Markets: Emerging markets will play an increasingly prominent role in global markets and economies, fueled by demographic trends, urbanization, and rising middle-class incomes. These markets will offer significant growth opportunities for businesses, particularly in sectors such as technology, healthcare, and consumer goods.

6. Regulatory Landscape: The regulatory landscape will continue to evolve in response to technological advancements, environmental concerns, and geopolitical tensions. Governments will grapple with issues such as data privacy, cybersecurity, antitrust enforcement, and climate change, shaping market dynamics and business strategies.

7. Geopolitical Uncertainty: Geopolitical tensions and trade disputes are likely to persist, creating uncertainty and volatility in global markets. Businesses will need to navigate geopolitical risks, trade barriers, and regulatory complexities as they seek to expand into new markets and manage global operations.

8. Changing Workforce Dynamics: The nature of work and employment will undergo significant changes, driven by automation, remote work, and the gig economy. Businesses will need to adapt to shifting workforce dynamics, invest in reskilling and upskilling initiatives, and embrace flexible and remote work arrangements to attract and retain talent.

In conclusion, the future of market dynamics promises to be both challenging and full of opportunities. By embracing technological innovation, sustainability, resilience, and agility, businesses can position themselves to thrive in a rapidly changing marketplace. By staying attuned to emerging trends, anticipating future developments, and adapting strategies accordingly, stakeholders can navigate the uncertainties of the future with confidence and success.

Conclusion

In conclusion, "Market Dynamics" has journeyed through the intricate interplay of factors shaping modern commerce. From the foundational principles of supply and demand to the nuanced realms of consumer behavior, technological advancements, regulatory changes, economic trends, globalization, and sustainability, each chapter has illuminated critical aspects of market dynamics. We've explored the intricate dance between competition and cooperation, witnessed the transformative power of innovation, and confronted the challenges of navigating an ever-evolving landscape.

As we reflect on the insights gleaned from these pages, one overarching truth emerges: the only certainty in the world of market dynamics is change itself. In an era defined by unprecedented disruption and rapid transformation, success hinges not on static formulas or rigid strategies, but on adaptability, resilience, and a relentless pursuit of innovation.

As readers embark on their own journeys in the dynamic world of business, may they carry with them the wisdom gleaned from these pages. May they embrace change as an opportunity for growth, navigate uncertainty with courage and clarity, and forge a path towards a future defined not by the constraints of the past, but by the boundless possibilities of tomorrow.

Ultimately, "Market Dynamics" serves not merely as a guidebook, but as a manifesto for those daring souls who dare to challenge the status quo, chart new horizons, and shape the destiny of markets yet to come. May its insights inspire, its lessons guide, and its wisdom empower all who seek to navigate the turbulent waters of commerce with vision, purpose, and unwavering resolve.

www.ingramcontent.com/pod-product-compliance
Lightning Source LLC
Chambersburg PA
CBHW082224220526
45470CB00010B/3302